Drought-Adapted Vine

Drought-Adapted Vine

POEMS BY

Donald Revell

Alice James Books

FARMINGTON, MAINE

Alice James Books are published by Alice James Poetry Cooperative, Inc.,
an affiliate of the University of Maine at Farmington.

Alice James Books
114 Prescott Street
Farmington, ME 04938
www.alicejamesbooks.org

Library of Congress Cataloging-in-Publication Data
Revell, Donald
    [Poems. Selections]
Drought-Adapted Vine : poems / Donald Revell.
    pages   ;   cm
    ISBN 978-1-938584-13-8 (softcover)
I. Title.
PS3568.E793A6 2015
811'.54--dc23   2015005079

Alice James Books gratefully acknowledges support from individual donors,
private foundations, the University of Maine at Farmington, and the
National Endowment for the Arts.

ART WORKS.
arts.gov

COVER ART: Bartram, William. Travels, 1793. Plate 27,
"Bartram's Evening Primrose." Courtesy of the Sterling Morton Library,
The Morton Arboretum.

CONTENTS

I

II

III

ACKNOWLEDGMENTS

I wish to thank the editors of the following for giving many of these poems their first appearance in print:

Academy of American Poets *Poem-a-Day*
American Poet
The American Poetry Review
Bat City Review
Catch Up
Conjunctions
Connotation Press: An Online Artifact
Fifth Wednesday Journal
The Literary Review
New American Writing
Postmodern American Poetry: A Norton Anthology (Second Edition)
Plume
Poetry
Unstuck
VOLT

FOR JAMES LONGENBACH

I

...what we changed
Was innocence for innocence...
—*The Winter's Tale*

Chorister

Cello or clarinet, it was smoke, smoke,
Just as Paradise fading over time at the road's
End is a black and white photograph
Of Paradise. Elementary schoolboy
Leaning into the hedgerow somehow still,
Such am I. A car passes. And then no
Traffic at all, for hours, for years it seems.
Make a little music, boy. Light a cigarette
Found in the roadway, a sign from God.
I remember the bitter taste of small berries
Before the summer began, and then
A bitter taste again in early autumn. Sweetness,
A little portion, like a wisp of smoke
Mistaken for music. A lonely car
Is all the traffic ever comes. Walk on.
I am entering a photograph fades with me
And no one else. Ahead, a derelict
Sound in the shape of cellos disappears
Into pale, gray foliage. Childhood's
Amazon River hounded out of church,
Out of the painfully small portion
Of ripe berries any soul can find,
Empties into Paradise one white boy.

3

A Shepherd's Calendar

A boy's face above a bicycle
One hour after sunrise
Riding west-south-west insists
Out of marred and moving whiteness
Wisdom consists entirely
Of afterwards, of far ahead
Where time is finished with itself
Just as the mountains over there
Are finished with the sun. For now,
Joy. For an hour at least,
The effortless white of the wheels.
Boy, to mar is to marvel.
To be the wound of the sun
On Time's face is beautiful.

Alphabet City: An Autobiography

AUGUSTINE
God is in the kitchen drawer,
And His love is infinite.

BEES
Are dying everywhere, and it
Will be the death of all gardens.

CHILDREN
Are bees.

DANTE
Has a box of crayons he'd like to share.

EVERYWHERE
There is one flower
Afraid of the sunlight.

FEAR
Desolates the colors,
Pigment of bees, pigment of children.

GUEVARA
Has a magical book. When
Someone reads it, she becomes a bird
No soldier can harm.

HEART
Is a hollow island
With hands of its own.
Those hands crush the heart.

ISOLDE
Is making her Christmas list
At the kitchen table. From time to time,
She pats the enormous dog at her feet.

JESUS
Held a buttercup beneath my chin.
There's no going back.

KENTUCKY
I'm just saying, in the middle of the night
I've seen horses thrown into fires,
And they were all praying together.

LOVE
Ask St. Augustine.

MIND
Not what I thought you were. I thought
You were myself, a step away. But no,
You are that crazy flower in Christ's hand.

NEW
York.

ORIGINAL
If only God had built a little house for Himself
Beside the apple tree and lived in it.

PLATO
Soccer cheese bum. I tried to teach my infant son to say
"Socrates is a bum."

QUIET
Not this side of extinction.

ROBERTA
Was my sister's name. It was she
Hung the bigger children on a fence for me.

SISTER
Come back.

TIME
Why can't we be friends? I remember one time
I was walking through Central Park and left
No footprints in the snow. We were friends that day,
Weren't we?

UNDERHILL
Was the name of our subway station,
Entirely above ground. It was also
Our telephone exchange.

VEINS
Little veins are bursting all over my legs
Like spiders bursting in the trees.

WHITMAN
Tell me, did you mean it? Is death really
As wonderful as you say?

XANADU

"Sloppy Joe's" sounds just about right. But still,
It would be foolish to forget that Coleridge
Was the best of us all.

YELLOW

The flowers have feasted upon bees and children.

Z

Alive still alive.

Beyond Disappointment

Ascending through yellow broom and sluggish
Red-brown wasps, I find the new house.
In no way does it resemble the old.
Let there be no comparisons then.
No kisses before or shirt-sleeves after.
I pull the comforter over my head,
And it is warm. The women spinning
In the next room weep as they spin.

Hence and farewell valediction: "life's journey."
It makes no sense. The children mock us with it.
A typewriter beneath the Christmas tree
Calls to the ice caps. Illustrated monthlies
Burn in the wasps' burnt nest. It is
Such perfections make the sun to rise.

In Paradise Alone

The very wasp of flowers is ago,
Almost ago; there's one, then one is two.
Some weeks from now, an hour
Writes it. Down in a book it goes,
Into the cluster, purple wings folded
Upon its breast which, after all, a shadow
Gnaws, knows. The one is two, distantly,
Never to know a wasp so close, a thing
As near as flowers. Time makes strangers.
The wind comes close to the ground, taking
Colors of bested soil into daylight.
The wasp unfolds. Flowers sing for joy,
"One at least! One at least!" Tatterdemalion my.

Letters to an English Friend

1.

No want of empire, only
Of wings, of true career.
Say mavis: match to strike.
Say threshing floor:
The republic evermore.

We are killing each other,
Not skating. These are
The last days and no
Kidding. The undersong
Perfected me, adored you.

Hart and hind, heart in hand.
William James places a white hand
Upon white Henry. The picture
Sets fire to the hair
Of two oceans.

2.

Wild fires out of control
In the ill spirit of
This summer's charity:
An election year, in-
Finite specimen hours.
Martin, you meant beauty
By wasps and lake water,

As I by dragonfly
And fires. Out of control,
Out of control and still
Not free. America
Rhymes all with algebra.
No wings for you or me.
No water for the fires.

3.

The loan is the Lazarus
Rain also saying late
Autumn into the tree

Whose one reply is
To flower to flower
Out of sequence as
There is no sequence now

Not any longer

Lazarus rhymes with Jesus
As James with Andrew
In between the syllables un–
Wind the winding sheet
Autumn comes again
Anymore hot for it hot

4.

Or lifts, as love was said to do, its shower.
It all comes round: Heraclitus, us;

Marvell, us; Hudson and Ouse.
I was thinking of death and of
Its curious elections. But love!
Unspoken illicit love in the lotos rose,
One and the same, is a shower too.

And so the visits to the grave
Are women, arms akimbo,
Smiles below ground. I
Will send a picture too, if you
Will call our river by a briar name,
Entire lifetimes in the swimmer's sound.

5.

Mine are the lesser trees
Nevertheless look upwards
Into the paloverde the topmost
Frivol branches a balloon
Blue for a boy my birthday
Remembered in heaven by
Christ of the lesser trees.

I cannot join you in Italy
But a Desert Father
A sort of fritillary noising
Balloon bellflowers only
This June morning gives me
An errand to give to you—
Taste two of the wines in Orvieto.

Which is the greener? Which is the color
Of summer straw after all the green has gone?

"Ridiculous winter flower"

Ridiculous winter flower
  More perfect butter

On the ground the disused
  Ground beloved

Must survive must live to tell
  Another orphan

Something raised us
  Out of the dust

Something gave us color
  A gold also tender

I shall not tell its name
  I'm tired

Laughter and piano teacher
  Ridiculous winter flower

The gate's wide open now

II

Is it a time to wrangle, when the props
And pillars of our planet seem to fail,
And Nature with a dim and sickly eye
To wait the close of all?
—WILLIAM COWPER, "*The Task*"

The Creation of the Stag

I dreamed the red chapel uncompleted, tall
In its iron graphic scaffolding.
Manhattan was two cities, and the chapel
Colored them red: birth and death; arrival
And departure. My mother was glad. Pointing
Up into the sky where a zodiac
Pinwheeled at her pleasure, she showed me
Taurus and Gemini, Scorpio
And Gemini covered in fresh paint.
Christ will stand there, just there, as today
Color and tiny, hazardous stars hang
Intervening fires. The middle of life
Is nothing. A nuclear pinfold frightens
Children frightened already. The chapel there
Rises above all of it, is a new deer.

.

Canary-yellow corduroy trousers
Embarrass the dream, as though a city
Were made of wine stains, red, my mother's wine,
The yellow of imagined birds
My father's disaster, his paint, his car.
The Gemini, with Taurus between them,
Smile. The chapel is in need of repair.
Smile. Rome was built in a day like today.
Only look into the sky to see
The pattern of God's pleasure—
Palette and planchette, color wheel—
Whose center never moves beneath the weight
Of the center. To the right is treason;
To the left, blindness. Between the Gemini,
Someone turns to ask: "Why are you crying?"

Here is a plate with an alphabet
Of flowers. Here is a zodiac.
I weep for the Gate of Kiev, for death
Saluting death with bells, backwards into
Things unfinished, like martyrdoms, from which
Cities arise only to be captured
By scaffolding. A man named Modest mourns
An architect called Victor. In the limousine
(For this is a procession—every poem
A procession) a pretty girl smokes. Outside
Of the car, clouds darken invisible
Windows. Cruelty is not a game here, not
A constellation. The swift stag from
Under ground bears up his branching head.
Too soon. Other animals must come before.

A change of address, from Arden to Paradise.
White-gold moonset, seraph of infinite
Compassion comes closest to me now:
At perigee, in white-gold May time, Taurus
Prevailing. At birth, the transparent
Scorpion feeds upon its mother.
The entire earth darkens to conceal
The terror. And still the seraph moon,
Though weary of me, weary of desert
Mountains that return no color, lingers
A sweet while. *Swete whilom.* Sweet William.
Stinking Billy, I heard the sound
Of a baseball falling into outstretched
Little hands. Here comes an animal.
Here comes the atomic bomb to old New York.

The day of my mother's funeral
The limousines were wild spiders
Trapped on a hillside, and we were inside
Them, waiting, waiting, only forsythia
Starry for hopeful, root and branch. Somehow the church,
In beautiful disrepair, appeared
Out of nowhere. I had chosen the wrong
Hymns, yet the sweet-faced Jamaican
Second-generation New Yorker
Priest officiating smiled and sang.
Outside, strangers filled the spiders
With yellow flowers. What is the use
Of cities, dead or alive? Simply,
That flowers are never out of place,
Never wrong. I have changed the address.

Redress. The priest deserves a better parish.
The bitter parish, Bemerton. And too,
The moon has seen enough. Of gullies,
Of loose dogs and walking bicycles,
Enough. Let everything fly. Let all
Angels become the angels of themselves.
Choosing the wrong hymns, choosing the right ones,
All on the color wheel for birthdays, one through five.
Geminiani selected five. With brides invisible, innumerable
In their bright ranks, the seraph of the evening sky
Welcomes my disrepair. Embarrassed by
The knowing smile of a sweet Jamaican,
I tell at last for the mean time my
Heart's truth. Eden is innumerable to me.
My eyes have been empty since childhood.

Care to try? Say that you were blind
And broke-necked, a city on the outskirts
With pears, with traffic, coffee regular sweet
Spittle on the pillow beside and underneath.
The pears are stranded, red and green. In Eden,
It was a yellow pear, with little windows
Cut into the flesh, too soon, too soon,
Flesh so bitter the wounds could not weep,
And so became windows. If I could turn
My head, I would see the heavy mourners
Holding coffee, stranded on the median,
In traffic. Lost to me now. Care to try?
One Chinese daughter. One imaginary boyfriend.
In the unfinished story, they live
Above a toy shop, one consummate lovely smile.

Of Satan and his dark materials,
Pandemonium of the colors, I
Can only say the human eye. Again,
As if I could lie beside my mother in the ground,
I say God made her eyes and mine to be
Travellers. We have garments. We have time.
And to every animal I now confide
An array of hours, a splendid vestment
Of hours, Alpha and Omega woven together.
You cannot tear me from my mother.
The stag bore up his branching head to travel
The universe, which is all forest, all earth,
All green with my mother's eyes. Where once
Constellations prowled menace and futurity,
Twin scorpions, I see a groundswell
Of time in the new birth, belling happiness.

You taught the book of life my name. Come, walk.
In the snow, it is 1978, on
Hertel Avenue, Buffalo, waiting
For you. Come. In the sunshine, earlier,
Pocket Shakespeare, Fort Tryon Park, New York,
On to the tree, onto the Trie Cloister.
Grandchild throws herself from the window
Only a little way to fall, rolling
Most of the way through the tall grass and down
Into Jewish flowers. I was reading.
I waited. It was Eden's reality
Proved unendurable. Flee, or be expelled.
The apple, Gemini, dreams likewise a Jew,
Before and after. Childhood is health,
Nature the white fiction we told ourselves.

Hurry so many animals. I must ask, while
The mornings are capable, while the grass
Is not ablaze or turned to black tailings.
Why is the chapel red? Why are the con-
Stellations, God's balloonists in the void,
Down to three? The color wheel, when
Did it become the destroyer of cities,
Mine especially, New York of the passengers?
Little enough to ride for free, little
Enough to ride your knee. Mother. Ruth
Amidst the alien pornography.
20 John 13—They have taken away
My Lord, and I know not where they have laid him.
Racist, greed-sick stalks of putrefaction,
They. My Pocket Shakespeare concedes the election.

I am the bird of the least morsel
Of your best memory. Speak to me,
Speak on behalf of me and to no one else.
I am the stag in the ruins. The great cities
Were dreams, red chapels of aberration
And the heartfelt error. The stag before,
The stag after, lifts up his branching head.
Creation considered of starlight long before,
When God had not yet made the world. As of today,
God has not yet made the world. Countless colors,
Countless colors, all of them eyes and eyebeams
Just now in your mouth at the point of sleep,
Catch fire. They have considered of starlight.
I see the lark not yet alighted upon
The animal, the soul before mine. Love.

III

I have drunk, and seen the spider.
— *The Winter's Tale*

To Shakespeare

He made a statue of the east wind
Reconciled never too late, in
Silhouette, never too late as these
First days of March turn backwards,
Facing the full of winter in
Enduring love, full jollity
Of winter's face to reconcilement,
In silhouette.

              He did not forget
Who lost his life to remember it.
Step down. Do not be proud.
There is a double heart behind
The breastbone. Bare it. Beat it.
Begin to eat it in full view,
Who loves you every inch of the wind.
First days of March, lords of jollity.

Debris

Antiquity shivers in the unbuilt tree.
She laments (antiquity is a widow, braided
Into the rained-upon color of desert trees
After a windstorm) her perfected dead.
The sound is keen, as though it were somehow calling
The windstorm back into its own debris.
Just so, it reaches me this Sunday morning,
Second of May, a day with no future but driving
Farther into the desert, into no mind
For anything but driving to the end
Of present days. The future is all fences,
Stray cats, and heroes walking backwards.
Antiquity shivers at the sight of me.

The Library

The library walks over fallen olives,
The tall library. Even as their shadows
Move, still leaves remain still. The passage
Of time is indescribable. Beloved
Songbirds are never far, but I forget them.

Stones stained by olives become white overnight.
Hearts stained by forgetfulness become white overnight.

Howling seven days in succession, the wind
Cannot stir a leaf. I believe in Heaven
Simply because there must be someone at one
O'clock in the morning who answers the phone.
The iron leaf of origin answers me.

They Are Not Making Anything.
They Are Working.

(Homage to Pierre Michon)

French for hatred, English for anger,
Black pony blinded, slender,
My secret Chaucer,
As for 60 years I've managed a lost river,
Water-jets over the lawns
In the last cool of a summer morning:
Cressid animal aube my daughter.

A cloud of thorns, acacia,
All that stands between us and bad Asia
Poised to kill with summer heat
Is the language, hatred and anger,
Blind caul of the vocables, lost river
To rhyme Daughter, Slender, Loire.
My secret Chaucer is a fatal mud, her new basilica.

Pitty-Pat

Oleander to the death of horses
Odilon Redon was mother's martyr
Ruined no mounted with true love but askew

How it is these sounds reach back in time
A first beloved smelling of milk and tar
In time to find first poets grassy

Churning the ice cream blossoming
Philosopher it makes sense it screams
Joy beloved joy and bees in the bedrooms

These sounds reach back in time I feel like an Indian
Like cut grass blown against the base of a mountain
I cannot share a dream we die alone

Born into such beautiful company
Foals find grass earth's countless eyes

Mountain's Edge

Misted sunlight, a scorpion
Fallen out of the sun
Covers the ground, all of it.
There is a rhythm to things,
But no help. So
Says the ruined poisoner.
We are here, here.
Sunlight answers to the call, and so too,
But tenderly, does Mr. Hart Crane.
Wasp-waisted scorpion
Fallen out of the sun
Must be grass, or otherwise
Be insane, building such a nest
In autumn, making God cruel.

France

France so small and awnings weeping
Carousel of crows my dear son
No suicide it is not church
It is home a happy brother
I had no brother until you

We found a pistol in the cornfield
You lifted it I lifted it
The sky became a tumult sky
God's broken eye I nearly said
Because it was weeping old souls

There are blue trains that go to France
When first I saw a yellow house
I lived in it begot a son
With nothing to sell I sold him

After Clare

Ball or balloon, beetle having torn
The wings from a fallen moth and called
Her kinsmen to the feast, so much
To be said is said in childhood, like
A pet name never to be heard again.
She left suddenly, with no explanation,
Never to be seen again.

I was away. I shall not forget,
But I shall surely be forgotten.
Love may come in its many disguises—
Son and daughter, dog and Beloved—
All the lost childhood without its tender name.

Ask me at Sunday School, as she did, about life,
And I will tell you again there is no such thing.

Borodin

When the world was loveliness I was
A composer, Borodin, my left eye
Level with the floor beside toy men.
Wild work and havoc they made
Being glad. I could draw a line
Would run straight through the minds of men
Being a sociable angel,
Music before and after, blushing.

Heaven is a nonsense entirely sensible.
I was a child on the floor beside you,
Making music, becoming small in the rosy
Embrace of God's best messenger.
I loved your havoc and your hair.

New Colors

The tree alive with invisible birds in no leaves
Is the soul of winter and says with Yeats
We wither into the truth whose truth is simply
That we die yet behind us the sky deepens
Into the deepest blue I mean to say that I
Could reach my hand forever into it
My hand would be covered with leaves and then
The birds would come in colors new colors
To robe archangels ruined back to life
We wither so to bear the weight of the invisible
Tell me shall I sing another cold day
Or is this merely the ruin before ruin
The shallow breath before no breath at all
Tell me is the sky behind me still

Tantivy

The late empurpl'd and dog's nostalgia
Ancient of days, only yesterday I had a
New sister. Kneel to crib, to chapel, a trip
To the moon. Sic semper my very first. Osip
Is older than he was. He died. He lay
Very close to a heap of goldfinches. Today
You spoke of my sister twice. Too far to go
Toys, reaching the bedroom toys like alto,
Almost, rhapsody of Brahms: never
Newly again in the late flowers, note of air.
Things breathe where I kneel. No matter whether
It rains or the chapel vanishes, they breathe.
Violets are the anniversary of something
Youthful covers the next hill hurrying.

Graves Variations

In Eden's garment, farthest heat and mistake,
We have reached the end of pastime, for always.
Single-minded midnight and noon agree:
No second chances. An epochal sun sees
Mountain ranges, and the mountains melt away.
In dreams, I return to mother's trellises and sex.
No flowers to be found, nor any angels
Barring the narrow path. Gladdest is
The garden that never was. Genesis
Makes nonsense of our Christmases.
Gladys is. Doris was. Leggy girls look up.
The mountains melt into a loving cup.

This morning, red racer or rattler
I cannot say, a beautiful serpent
Died where I wasn't looking, in the yellow
Doorway. Had it followed me? Hunted me?
These questions, bird, are not rhetorical.
It was crushed below the heart and died slowly.
Yellowhammer, you saw it all and kept
The flicker of your dull song aloft.
Serpent Beethoven. Yellowhammer late quartet.
I would add "etcetera," but this is not
Rhetorical. It reeks pure mystery, the only
One of its kind, poor beast of next and nil.

Look forward, truant, to your second childhood.
Meanwhile, left behind, I am left to sell
A ragtag legend of Creation to the remnant.
Try the door handle. Try it. If it opens at all,
There is only smoke and the apparition
Of mother or of Anticlea or boys
Nodding off into the sleep which hates sleep.
Cain slew Abel with a Christmas tree.
Odysseus died en route. As for me,
A serpent is my bicycle and mother.
Factor into Paradise the nil
Of kisses. It opens briefly, if it opens at all.

I have a calling to marry children, myself
Among them. And why set miracles apart?
Attentions, as if with sweets and cutlasses,
Climb the sky. Out of their little houses
Clamber the green kids. Fleeting brushstroke
Heads, fleeting brushstroke arms and legs,
They climb the sky. Not enchanted but faithful
To a tree that God forbade and planted in them,
They marry in the leaves. They marry in thunderheads
And in pinpricks of starlight. The painter
Finds them heaped in one body, his and mine.
The very next Cadillac is candy red.

Clothed in Eden's garments, I find candy
Easy to come by. Immortality
Without flowers is a better sleep
Than madcap syllables, than the kissing bijou.
God, at last, has taken me at my word.
He has taken the green jewels out of my eyes,

And they are eyes once more. He has bound my mind
Onto a wheel—wheeeeeee! Ixion or Gladys
Gladdest is. To die with a forlorn hope,
But soon to be raised, reeks pure mystery
And proves a mountain in me, white earth
Beloved of aspen trees twinned at birth.

Deluge

I'd like for poetry to die with me:
Not only mine, but all of it. Where's
A good word now for *Louis Quinze*?
Can symmetries survive themselves?
Can the shadows of trees so razor-edged
At the fingertips of untouched women
Possibly survive a single winter,
Much less the oblivion humanity
Justly mistakes for simple change? The nearest heat
Is far. Horses refuse Phaeton.
Awake before anyone, untouched women
Slowly cleanse the body of a day
Never to dawn. In the east, horizon
Unwrites itself in momentary raiment:
Reddish-gold that blackens into mountains.

IV

…this is an art
Which does mend nature, change it rather, but
The art itself is nature.
— *The Winter's Tale*

The Watteau Poem

Life in heaven not alto, but the freight
Train's higher register a shriek of couplings
In the February night air bedside
Table bedside telephone 1982
Resembles her, resembles the two of us.
We are an old married couple in Corinth,

Tennessee. How is any child's
Eyesight a heaven? Any soprano
Stepping down out of the cars onto?
The color of periwinkles not yet
Came very soon afterwards, palette.
Be easy in your mind. Read yourself to sleep.

Into a train yard cauldron one man,
Watteau until later on, looks again.

Corinth, Tennessee is a township northeast of the city of Knoxville.

Symphony No. 4 of Gustav Mahler includes the song "Das himmlische Leben" for solo soprano.

Periwinkles, in French "pervenches, blue flowers of the dogbane family, Apocynaceae."

Jean-Antoine Watteau, October 10, 1684–July 18, 1721. Rococo?

A sudden river to the clown of roses,
S-curved presidency, the letters too
Are letters, and I mean to say Pierrot
Run among the roses suddenly red.
What's to be said for understanding? Too
Late, too late. Those saints won't hunt. These flowers
Understand nothing of the waking sleep
Makes poetry. How many red letters
In a country mile? We cross the river
Simply to rest in the shade of things, curved
In a flash and onrush I can feel,
Sleeping with you. Almost sleeping. I see
A garden scripted beneath our breath and noise.
See here, Johanna, Joachim, and Watteau!

Another will entice me on, and on
Through almond blossoms and rich cinnamon;
Till in the bosom of a leafy world
We rest in silence, like two gems upcurl'd
In the recesses of a pearly shell. (John Keats, "Sleep and Poetry")

Let us cross over the river and rest under the shade of the trees. (Last words of Stonewall
Jackson, May 10, 1863)

Yes, I can hear it. Inside
The tiger lily bent double,
What I'd taken for a soft breeze:
Bee mouth, behemoth, sips. It is
For you to decide. The beauty
Bent to the breaking point, is she
Sad? Is she Cythera? Turn, turn
To me, and I shall honestly.

What Watteau? If ever I once
Breathed the fine air, Dumbarton Oaks,
The world premiere of another
Country, June 1984,
The waitress is in love with us.
Are we the exact pilgrims? Yes.

The Embarkation for Cythera, painted by Watteau, 1717. The beautiful pilgrims, have they only now departed? Have they only now arrived?

Another Country, a British film written by Julian Mitchell and adapted from his play of the same title. Part romance, part historical drama, it is based upon events in the early life of Guy Burgess, spy and double-agent. Betrayal is a sacrament of the last man, of the priest unto himself alone.

Dumbarton Oaks. Bliss family estate in Washington, DC. The house is now a museum and research library. The extensive gardens, designed by Beatrix Farrand, are open to the public.

If the horse any longer…it was you.
Ride it. Restore the original word
Inside an only. And here it comes clattering,
The matter once only and, afterwards,
God.
       I'd arranged a shelf of animals.
At the center was a clear space,
An ark for snow, dust, and adagios.

Comes a time you must understand, you two,
I did it for you. I left my lover
On the far side of the swimming horses.
Chincoteague, Cythera, the summer house
I never saw builded, although I am
The spook of the builders, Antoine Watteau.

Chincoteague Island is a coastal island in Accomack County, Virginia. The horses
known as "Chincoteague Ponies" actually live and graze on the salt marshes of
nearby Assateague Island, and are descended from animals released into the wild by
17th-century British colonists. On the last Wednesday of every July, riders herd some
of the ponies and swim them across the narrow channel to Chincoteague, where they
are auctioned off in aid of the local Fire Department. Once, in Colorado, a cowboy
poet asked me if I'd ever seen horses eating fish out of the ocean. I think of the
Chincoteague Ponies as of angels, as of tireless commuters, as recovering alcoholics
in a story by John Cheever. I would like to walk beside one across the Tappan Zee
Bridge some early morning, whistling the adagio from Brahms' violin sonata in G
major. In 1861, the residents of Chincoteague Island voted not to secede from the
Union.

A place of quiet nor of such consent
Never any of it turning to say
The perfect life is ourselves this evening
Once the weight the desperation of it
Intoxicated as the mountain lights
Nearest buildings some distance away mark
Events of such glamor loves our waitress

Wanting to care to bring us the mountain
Alphabet of which your green eyes show
There is no cutting corners in color
The heaven-sent harries our evidence
Each sign each second of extremity
All rescued by the Lord gives freely
Unhappy we cannot say He

In celebration of the 300th anniversary of Watteau's birth, a major retrospective of his
works was assembled. It travelled to several of the world's great museums, including
the National Gallery of Art in Washington, DC where it was on display from 17 June
through 23 September 1984. I saw it there. Betrayal hung upon the face of Watteau's
Pierrot (sometimes known as Gilles) like a cloudy veil upon a weathered mask.
Earlier that summer, in New York, at the Whitney Museum, I'd seen a retrospective
of the paintings of Fairfield Porter. The clouds in Maine, the houses beneath them,
the lawns running down to the ocean, shone separately, each from the other, in
distinctive, pious illumination. The parts of a world are alone with God, crowded
together. I can never separate the Watteau exhibition, in memory, from the Fairfield
Porters I'd seen a few days earlier, some distance to the north. Columbine might have
been a dog asleep in Maine. Harlequin remained hidden somewhere in an upstairs
bedroom.

Blaze of fir along the ground, I mean
Needles in a finger-splay showing
God's direction to the wind, why now?
Could it not have saved the boy sooner?
Colin to Cuddie: blow the fire.
Love to liking: lullay my dear one.

Rummage the odes for a fir tree more,
A black finger mark on pitch-black sky.
I will lug my son into the light
Soon. Blaze me then. If the ground envies
The wind, despair's a fine thing. Mine eyes
Etcetera will lug my son soon.

Pagans were underfoot always, Watteau,
Heavy to me and not a boy for you.

———————————

Colin Cloute, a shepheardes boy enamor'd of Rosalind. Colin is Edmund Spenser's own
avowed persona in The Shepheardes Calender. A rural musician and lay-prophet,
Colin is the conscience of English pastoral poetry, forever and ever.

Cuddie, an unhappy Heardsmans boye. Cuddie is the main character of Spenser's
"Februarie" eclogue.

*Lullay, myn lykyng, my dere sone, myn swetyng, / Lullay, my dere herte, myn owyn dere
derlyng.* Fifteenth-century English Christmas carol.

Then you, the burlesque of our lust—and faith, / Lug us back lifeward—bone by infant bone.
Hart Crane, "National Winter Garden."

Of smoke in Bethel, no solitude can say,
Or archangel. Said Christ to me a wisp
Tilted into the trees to meet mountains,
Palm trees. Company of losels and pricks.
Say it again, Lord. We are not lonely.

Asking girls at two o'clock in the morning
Stabbed through the heart, joy's absolute only
Saying, will you be married all these years?

Bejeweled, yes, where the dog was sick.
Heaven's gate, yes, made of pearl and jasper.
Also I had in my mind the fountain
Wept a crazy glass into my birthday.
A new car is another Christmas morning
Farther on. Further, Antoine, my roundelay.

Bethel, literally "House of God." In Genesis, Bethel is the site of Jacob's dream, the
dream of a ladder thronged with angels ascending and descending. In my Sunday
School, we read very little of the Old Testament, and so it was not until I came across
Denise Levertov's beautiful 1961 collection that I knew anything of that dream. I
never met Denise, but we did have a good correspondence over the course of several
years, from 1986 until her death. Her letters seemed always to arrive when I most
needed them. They were like the windows of houses in paintings by Vuillard.

Losels, scoundrels, good-for-nothings, rogues.

Jasper, Revelation 21:18, "And the building of the wall of it (Jerusalem) was of
jasper..." Among the secrets of why and why now, I ask you to number the death of
our dog Jasper, a giant schnauzer.

A space between clockwork and the rainbow
Wrapped in wads of hay, happens a child.
Whose? Mary would say Cupid's. Venus would
Paint rainbows across my Christ, the soar
Falcon I should learn. And so it is
Star's lief to wander, murdering as far
As the next animal—hind, bee—nightgowned
For the fayre election, calling itself
Queenie. Children hurt one another
And themselves. Between the clockmaker God,
Combing the beaches, and His joy fell a truth
Like thousands of wounds. Watteau, it's Christmas!
The elementary school playgrounds
Behave the night sky as if they owned it.

Covenant below my eye, self-made
Something, dread awhile to frighten rabbits
Out of the snow, but no, nothing like that,
I went to the window today nearly blind.

Christ promised me American catastrophe
All my own. My erst friends, beloved,
Would hurry away down the white, white snow,
And I would pound into the window panes

White names, their names. Below the eye, self-made
Imagination of a colored spree
Plays hangman. Wretched man. Wretched tree.
Ermine of the coldest kind, says Watteau.

Into my heart to write a Christ did, once,
The whole way go, on the off chance.

Window panes facing onto a little square of garden, Saturday, October 13, 1984, a
letter on my desk from a dear friend thanking me for happy days in Washington—
Dumbarton Oaks, the Watteau exhibition, a screening of "Another Country."

Wretched tree—I am thinking of the elder tree. Adultery is the good health of human
helplessness every time, every time, and also of its hair and Harlequin.

A fold field chose The rightest boy
Something to wings Well-accustomed
So that so that A long woman
Finding him nude Would love and know
The carrying Beneath her heart
Was his was he A fold field chose

In the Grecian Epigraphy
Muddle is made Of a plain truth
As if two girls Climbing a hill
To some ruins Were not two girls
And the long boy Trailing after
Were not the Christ But one Greek more

Christ's epigone Clownish Watteau
Painted for them A hilltop home

Epigraphy is the study of inscriptions, and particularly of ancient inscriptions.

Epigone: an undistinguished imitator or follower; also *Epigon,* one born after; in the plural, *Epigoni,* as in the sons of The Seven against Thebes.

…Time is the steward of décor.
In auctioned fittings that no longer are,
Persists the image that forever is:
Ease, class on class, and in the distance, war. ("Epigoni Go French Line" by Turner Cassity)

I met Turner Cassity only once, at the home (27 Chestnut Street, Binghamton NY) of Patricia Wilcox, sometime in the spring of 1974. His patter was devilish and keen and kind: "Why do the wicked proper, Patty? *Because* they are wicked!" Patricia Wilcox was the first friend my writing ever had, and certainly the best. She perfectly loved this world of which she perfectly despaired. God's truth was an oxalis growing in her kitchen window. I last visited her and her family in June 1984, right around the time of my 30th birthday.

Very light snow of smalls. The last one,
Time at last to praise intervals when
Nightclothes, speaking of angels, begin
In cold beloved bed one flannel,
Falls. Afterwards there must be skating.
Lately, Watteau, I've found you often
Painting flannel and periwinkle
In the 23rd psalm. Is it me?

It is small enough to pray, and cold
In bed. Cupped in blue flowers, needle-
Sharp as winter starlight, the breasts of
Skating you know. The musics will stray.
Periwinkle and dots of fire
Praise Christ Cupid on snowy rapier.

This morning of the small snow/I count the blessings… (Charles Olson, "The Songs of Maximus")

The Bishop's Wife, a film (1947) directed by Henry Koster and adapted from Robert Nathan's novel of the same name. In the scene I'm remembering, the angel Dudley (played by Cary Grant) is seated on the floor beside a child, the Bishop's little daughter. He tells her a story of a shepherd boy's fight with a lion, and the story becomes Psalm 23. The scene is so deeply focused, so clear and clean-edged, it could only have been photographed by Gregg Toland, as indeed it was. Cinematographer of *Wuthering Heights, The Grapes of Wrath,* and *Citizen Kane,* Toland died in 1948 at the age of forty-four.

Tan-ta-ra cries Mars on bloody rapier,
Fa-la, fa-la, fa-la, cries Venus in her chamber.
Toodle loodle loo, cries Pan that cuckoo,
With bells at his shoe, and a fiddle too. (Thomas Weelkes, 1608)

How near would you dare to row? Revisit
Your island now after so many such
Mornings, mornings the rabbits set to burst
Cornflower blue, is it smoke, is it frost
So makes the color, and you would surely
Never leave. Her. You once together set
The lintel askew from a ship's last timber.
Her. And the animals came to your hand.

The color of foam is sound, not color.
Swale, gunnel, swamp Andromeda, choose, man,
You must choose your parcel of imagined
Land and live in it, dry, berry-brown dry.
Dressed as a clown Antony, Antony
Rows for home. Christmas, they said. Come Christmas.

...I put the idea to the Steward, who sent for rabbits from Neuchatel, both bucks and does, and we proceeded in great ceremony, his wife, one of his sisters, Therese and I, to install them on the little island, where they were beginning to breed before my departure and where they will doubtless have flourished if they have been able to withstand the rigours of winter. (Jean-Jacques Rousseau, *Reveries of the Solitary Walker*, trans. Peter France)

Entirely forgotten they the license, hame and sky.
To manage a fine staircase, turning one's eyes
To his angels of no help, needing any, they
Have forgotten. Take this engine now from me.
Beloved rib cage and poverty hame.
Bell. Bell. Steeple that buried my parents
Under the hill was a staircase too.

Psyche had two sisters. Of women, a man
May speak to facts but never to opinion.
I was given a flag at my father's grave.
Beside him, my mother in death has made
A baroque staircase, a variance, a rage
Brighter than archangels. Take it from me.
Totty as busy rain, climb it, climb it.

"...no unearned income/can buy us back the gait and gestures//to manage a baroque staircase, or the art/of believing footmen don't hear/human speech."—W.H. Auden, "Thanksgiving for a Habitat"

Psyche Showing her Sisters her Gifts from Cupid, painting by Fragonard, 1753 (collection of the National Gallery, London).

"Yes, I will be thy priest and build a fane/In some untrodden region of my mind,/Where branched thoughts, new grown with pleasant pain,/Instead of pines shall murmur in the wind..."—John Keats, "Ode to Psyche"

Busyrane: a wizard in Spenser's The Faerie Queene. Busyrane was associated with lust and with sexual love.

Watteau in rags: climb! For only far is
Free. The difference between a rag and a rapier
Catches fire at extreme of sky,
Disappearing just then, sex then, leaving
Adam there, Eve until a long time
Mother mine. The baroque smiles across me.
Edna Davis pray for me and my good conduct.

Sainted depth of focus undercroft pray.
All over again shall we manage
The staircase, a ways ahead,
Rags becoming rage, brightness falling through
Busy rain. June 18th, 1961.
The final license of a final day
Says you. And of the two sisters, one says I.

At my right hand always, when I am writing, sits *The Hymnal of the Protestant
Episcopal Church in the United States of America* (1940) inscribed in delicate blue
handwriting,

For good conduct
From, Edna Davis
(Teacher)
June 18, 1961

V

A serious prophet upon predicting a flood should
be the first man to climb a tree.
—*The Red Badge of Courage*

Olney Hymn

not my li-
fe this and
that is a
death I can-
not die
O'Neill
doesn't even
know me
any old lady
on a porch
with a pill
shows me the
rain begin-
ning its godly
amble up
the green al-
ley my life
rain rain
on the chain-
link fences
on the ragged
red leaves
and green in-
visible flowers
my three
children em-
bracing me
brush the hand-
print of God
from my shirt

this and that
and that is
a death I can-
not die

For John Riley

The murdered poet opens to a torn page.
A ridiculous gesture, save for being true.
Mow the grass and the dragonflies feast.
Water the grass and birds feast.
North of England mariachi ampersand.
The enjambed trees make enormous portals.

Go apple, apfel, apples fall in parallel,
Each alone. Likeness is no likeness nor
Contrast a divide. The Holy Ghost
Proves God a murderer. I am on Christ's side,
Horizontal with the slain whose shadows
Keep the grass together. Keep walking.

Worlds apart are all the worlds we know.
I lifted the skirts of childhood to say so.

Black Madonna

The day is mountains, too many mountains.
Counting them, I see that something happens
Between three and four. Black Madonna counts
The fingers and enigmas of her newborn son.
Lady, push the old car out of the snow,
The snow's turning black. I hate to see it.

And when he is grown and I am gone,
The man is a trouble in the trees, not
One of us and not a part of me.
This now, this then, and this shape of animals
Striding across the end of time
As mountains, make sounds. To count them all

Is to become Christ. Snow comes after,
Like sweat in the music between three and four.

The Cattle Were Lowing

It might also have been a sleigh ride.
Mozart's sister, a perfect oval and more
  than perfect incline,
Tucked into a blanket, laughs
For the first and last time in her life.

Genealogies tickle a little, and then a long
  pain afterwards—
Pain of connection, most awful
Pain of separation every Christmas.
Even angels find their armor
  burdensome then.

We rode across the snowy plain. The earth
Was mirror-glass ground into a fine powder.
Oh do not stop. Do not stop ever. I
Will give you a book of matches if...

There is the first of three dances still to consider,
And poverty, sole purpose of the wren.

Hunting

A cloud, a rabbit, and a quail, these
Are the letters of Jesus' name.

Ewer,
Dogs and a ewer:
Vermeer angers your awful roommate,
And still God's mercy rains upon the past.

Put it together.
Donald, only you.
Vermeer—
Dogs and a ewer.

Either everything is music or nothing is.
Either we live in the past or there are more birds
Than can be counted.
Everything is music.

Gihon

They all wore little hats
Vermont that I
Can see, the river its coronet
Of yellow beetles—crawling,
Flying—the flowers wearing
The river for a hat.
I can see that
When I stand alone
Upon this acre as now
Sober and living, the same, the same.

They wore:
Hats.
They are not dead,
John and Johnny and John,
Which is a fine name for a river,
Only gone.
Having death out of the way,
The ill-fitting suicide discarded,
Pajama-like, on imaginary sand:
Good, good. We stand.

Air and Angels

What if they knew.
We shall unearth them,
Drink the alcohol from their matted hair.
Unclosing their eyes, we shall perhaps
Find that final retinal flare
Of the angel or eruption
Into new life of a birthing star.

Breathless is the word.
Comes a time there is no other sound
But intake, but inspiration
That tilts my head into an empty cloud.
The animal finds a way to the window.
The soul, in one last fling of desolation,
Dives underground where it must not go.

To Heaven

The working class is not a leaf. The leaves are leaves.
In oval portraits, child by child, the entire innocence
Of the world shrinks to nothing. Geminiani gone.
Dante done to death. I dreamed of a forest where my skin
Was gray and my loves were gray and all the leaves
Were golden. It was as good as an ocean.
No one said a word. There was nothing to explain.

I wake each morning much too early. The low moon
Accuses. The distant traffic noises and first airplanes
Accuse. I reach for my glasses in the half-light hoping
For a moment or two with the ovals by my bed.
There is a distant nude who was a baby. There are two
Children reaching upwards towards a golden leaf.
In forests hereafter, they take me back to sleep.

Encantadas

Poisonous flower of the soul obscene rigging
Of tall ships tattooed onto blue water tattooed
Flesh of the soul Richard of Saint Victor told you
The body is inside the soul a-sail westward
To the islands of flowers and we shall be there
Early tomorrow we shall have awakened pure
From dreams of ourselves nude stranded in the rigging
Richard of Saint Victor has uttered prayers westward
From the black Encantadas rest safely darling
Put your faith into the clouds these white sheets sailing
Entire worlds early souls aweigh poisonous
Irises with wings I mean the ground is alive

Foxglove

I saw the grass giving live birth to grass,
Every blade open, pushing new,
Wet clumps into the light. I saw
Funnel clouds buried in the ground teeming
With young fish. There were also children
Running around with brightly colored pails.
Imagine what they did. It was springtime.

Vision runs up a hill called Vision. It never
Comes down. A religion of balloons stays aloft
A long time, long enough at least to cross over
Into non-conforming grassland—a reindeer,
Craggy, milkmaid running for her life land.
And poetry. Jesus please slow down.
The bad men are far behind us now.
Lunching among postcards of the Last Judgment,
We can breathe. We have time. We have plenty of it.

BOOK BENEFACTORS

Alice James Books wishes to thank the following individuals who generously contributed toward the publication of *Drought-Adapted Vine*:

Kazim Ali

For more information about AJB's book benefactor program, contact us via phone or email, or visit alicejamesbooks.org to see a list of forthcoming titles.

Refuge/es, Michael Broek
O'Nights, Cecily Parks
Yearling, Lo Kwa Mei-en
Sand Opera, Philip Metres
Devil, Dear, Mary Ann McFadden
Eros Is More, Juan Antonio González Iglesias, Translated by
    Curtis Bauer
Mad Honey Symposium, Sally Wen Mao
Split, Cathy Linh Che
Money Money Money | Water Water Water, Jane Mead
Orphan, Jan Heller Levi
Hum, Jamaal May
Viral, Suzanne Parker
We Come Elemental, Tamiko Beyer
Obscenely Yours, Angelo Nikolopoulos
Mezzanines, Matthew Olzmann
Lit from Inside: 40 Years of Poetry from Alice James Books, Edited by
    Anne Marie Macari and Carey Salerno
Black Crow Dress, Roxane Beth Johnson
Dark Elderberry Branch: Poems of Marina Tsvetaeva, A Reading by
    Ilya Kaminsky and Jean Valentine
Tantivy, Donald Revell
Murder Ballad, Jane Springer
Sudden Dog, Matthew Pennock
Western Practice, Stephen Motika
me and Nina, Monica A. Hand
Hagar Before the Occupation | Hagar After the Occupation, Amal al-
    Jubouri
Pier, Janine Oshiro
Heart First into the Forest, Stacy Gnall
This Strange Land, Shara McCallum
lie down too, Lesle Lewis

ALICE JAMES BOOKS has been publishing poetry since 1973.
The press was founded in Boston, Massachusetts as a cooperative
wherein authors performed the day-to-day undertakings of the
press. This collaborative element remains viable even today, as
authors who publish with the press are also invited to become
members of the editorial board and participate in editorial
decisions at the press. The editorial board selects manuscripts for
publication via the press's annual, national competition, the Alice
James Award. Alice James Books seeks to support women writers
and was named for Alice James, sister to William and Henry,
whose extraordinary gift for writing went unrecognized during
her lifetime.

DESIGNED BY MIKE BURTON

∴

PRINTED BY THOMSON-SHORE